BOA
EDITIONS
LIMITED

OFF-SEASON IN THE PROMISED LAND

Off-Season
in the Promised Land

POEMS BY
Peter Makuck

AMERICAN POETS CONTINUUM SERIES, NO. 95

BOA Editions, Ltd. ❧ *Rochester, NY* ❧ *2005*

First Edition
05 06 07 08   7 6 5 4 3 2 1

Publications by BOA Editions, Ltd.—
a not-for-profit corporation under section 501 (c) (3)
of the United States Internal Revenue Code—
are made possible with the assistance of grants from
the Literature Program of the New York State Council on the Arts;
the Literature Program of the National Endowment for the Arts;
the Sonia Raiziss Giop Charitable Foundation; the Lannan Foundation;
the Mary S. Mulligan Charitable Trust; the County of Monroe, NY;
the Rochester Area Community Foundation;
the Elizabeth F. Cheney Foundation; the Ames-Amzalak Memorial Trust
in memory of Henry Ames, Semon Amzalak and Dan Amzalak;
the Chadwick-Loher Foundation in honor of Charles Simic and Ray Gonzalez;
the Steeple-Jack Fund; the Chesonis Family Foundation,
as well as contributions from many individuals nationwide.

See Colophon on page 96 for special individual acknowledgments.

Cover Design: Daphne Poulin-Stofer
Cover Photo: Justin Brett
Interior Design and Composition: Richard Foerster
Manufacturing: McNaughton & Gunn, Lithographers
BOA Logo: Mirko

Library of Congress Cataloging-in-Publication Data

Makuck, Peter, 1940–
    Off-season in the promised land : poems / by Peter Makuck.— 1st ed.
        p. cm. — (American poets continuum series ; v. 95)
    ISBN 1–929918–71–2 (pbk. : alk. paper)
    I. Title. II. Series.

PS3563.A396O34 2005
811'.54—dc22

2005017456

BOA Editions, Ltd.
Thom Ward, Editor
David Oliveiri, Chair
A. Poulin, Jr., President & Founder (1938–1996)
260 East Avenue, Rochester, NY 14604
www.boaeditions.org

for Brendan Galvin

Paradise is where I am
　　　　　　　—Voltaire

Contents

PART I

Departures

At Island Harbor
boats have been hauled.
An empty pier points across the sound

to the Intercoastal,
a parade of migrating motor yachts and schooners,
a few bright sails.

Red admirals,
sulfurs, painted ladies, and monarchs
flutter in low light

over elaeagnus and late lantana
and don't seem to know
where Mexico is,

Charleston, Savannah, or Key West.
The light is perfect
and long shadows flare from the pilings.

When plankton dies,
the water clears like a mind.
Blueclaws disappear over ribs of sand.

The ocean deepens
to an unkeepable blue.

Off-Season

All day the ocean's been burning
a cold blue that matches my mother's willowware,
the few cracked cups that I've kept.

I've come along a path through the dunes
to listen to the water's drunken repetitions—
that story about the *Wendy Lee,*
how she went down in rough weather last week,
four mothers made into widows.

Just off the bar, there's a shrimper hauling nets,
red and green running lights,
a Christmas tree in the oncoming dark.

A string of black scoters angles to the south, skims
a surface still lit with a last brandy tinge.

A scatter of sandpipers
works the beach in winter white, unbothered
by immensity, all dash and wistful peep.

I've wallowed in this windy emptiness before,
feeding a feeling that won't go away,
and won't become something else—a voice
you once loved, her hand on your cheek,
the way your father squinched his eyes when he laughed.

But reunion doesn't happen like this.
No lambent figures looming through cheap-effect mist
with a password that opens
the radiant purpose of all things.

What do I want? I know about the lost,
what search and rescue means—
every small thing is a clue. A single light comes on
in the long curve of off-season houses.

A pelican hangs overhead.

The shrimper is disappearing
but I still see a mate in dim light working the cull.
Gulls squall and flicker in the half dark.
Something invisible wants to be seen.

Empty Air

Twilight and snowflakes are falling at the same time
whitening the empty street in front of our house

and the shortcut through Wilson's woods
that took me to the older boys on Clifton Street.

Our breaths looked like smoke
and lights came on in houses down the hill.

Mothers called from porches and
one by one our players left the game.

Now just Benny and Gary and me.
Gary spun the ball on his fingertip,

looked around, and said: *Practice time.*
Pete, go long and deep. On three.

Benny would hike. I knew the route.
Sprint down the right side to the culvert,

then zig to the middle where
Gary's great arm would have the football

spiraling down to my outstretched hands.
But, when I turned, the air was empty and

so was the street. Not even muffled laughter,
just snowflakes that are falling.

In the woods toward home, I stopped on the path.
Snow crystals ticked in the leaves. I stood there

for a long moment, not wanting a thing . . .

Portside Marina

On an outer pier, one of the floaters,
I'm flat on my belly, face near the water,
knuckles bleeding, scraped
on the bilge pump I couldn't repair
with pliers or curses.
Howling and hitting the piling
with a hammer
made me entertainment
for the beer-drinking captains
passing binocs in the office: *Check 'im out—*
That ol' boy's ready for the rubber room.

Then it comes to me,
either grace
or too much lunch wine,
and I sag to my knees
with a half-eaten drumstick on a string.
I'm almost a boy again,
my frowning face
mercifully clouded by minnows.

I'm nearing something deep
as the ocean itself,
equalizing, breathing myself closer,
just inches down,
down to this floating dock reef
with its amber algae, long and hairlike,
barnacles, polyps

and minnows quick
and thick on the drumstick
at a game of bump and tug,
a cloud of glints,
then a rock bass and a blue crab

up from their dark lurk
easy as words.

But I lift the bone
to slow things down,
Patience, patience,
and I'm diving
on an offshore wreck
with Dave who shows me this trick
with his knife:
he pries a purple urchin loose
from the wheelhouse roof,
then chops it open and,
as if conjured,
dozens of spot-tails with violet ventrals
billow around us, curve and lace,
a ballet of slow breathing
in this church light
that is always available.

Promised Land

First sails of the season patch and color the bay.
My skiff tugs at its lines, antsy to be elsewhere

as I talk to the dock master, an old-timer
who knows this whole necklace of islands

like his right hand, rough as a barnacled hull.
He tells me how little by little on Shackleford,

the next island east, they cut down trees
for houses and boat wood, and how they

cut their own throats at the same time.
Sand traveled, barrier dunes came down,

and when the big blow hit, wash-over
killed all the gardens and wells. No going back.

In less than two years, wild horses
had the island all to themselves.

Some families dug up their dead
and took boxes of bones when they fled.

His granddaddy floated and sailed their house
to the mainland, Promised Land,

they call it, a few waterfront blocks in the city.
But look around, he says. It's happening here:

Down with the live oaks, up with the condos!
Years ago, out at the point—hell, what's the use?

Shakes his head, says he knows what I'm thinking:
The older you get, the better it was. But it *was*.

Now he sketches a map to the old burial ground,
and puts X's where sunken timbers mine the way,

explains how to find the old ferry channel
that every year travels with shoaling:

Tip up your lower unit and prop.
Ease ahead slow. Feel your way

and watch your depth—what you don't see
can take you straight to the bottom.

Dominion

Just off the blacktop
there's a silver marker,
black letters flaking:

Union Forces
under General John G. Parke
landed here
on March 29, 1862
in the Fort Macon Campaign.

In no time it hits you
that the "here" has moved,
retreated from a union
of greater forces—winds and tides
that sanded in the landing
and shoved the water
half a mile north,
the island in steady
advance on the mainland.

But the "here" now waits
for another defeat.
You can see for yourself,
become a rebel,
leave your car
in the Food Lion lot,
and hike down a sandy track
to Hoophole Creek,
a limbed-over tunnel
that at last opens
on the cordgrass flats,
wading birds, an adagio
of clouds, wide water, and sky.

But first take your time
in the grove of grandfather oaks,
those widespread limbs
dangling long mosses
of confederate gray.
It's thick shade, hard to see
at first the hot pink
fluttering from pounded stakes,
or belted around trunks
nailed in transit crosshairs
that will forever defeat

a place famous
to a few fishermen,
crabbers and birders
who can walk down a path
where flycatchers
and kingbirds dart
through the half-light
and skirmish in an airy here.

General Parke took the fort.
Out of the north
a phalanx of dark clouds.
Hoophole flutters with deadly pink.
Only now is the same
and always that hunger
for dominion.

Minding What's There

I'm browsing shell beds
and trying to work through
the one about who we are
when we forget to practice
who we are,

only half aware of the ocean
taking itself seriously,
a tall white tumble and hiss.
I should know the ebb
from flood by sound alone

but it's a clump of sea foam,
stranded and iridescent,
like an enlightened mind,
that tells me
about the effort of arrival.

Shells crackle underfoot,
bits of scallops and olives,
whelks and razors,
then a black isosceles
bigger than an arrowhead

stops my restless ramble
and has me stoop.
Two inches from base to tip,
shiny as obsidian, and sharp—
edges themselves tiny teeth,

a dark design, perfect
for ripping and sawing,
changed only in color
since fallen eons ago
from a jawful of others.

Its edge draws
a bead of blood on my arm,
those zigzag fins
beyond the surf zone at dusk,
sometimes an attack—

that girl we taunted
in high school ages ago
with "Sharkey,"
her sidelong glance
and crooked teeth.

I let it fall into the dark
of my pocket, testing
its edge with my thumb,
climb from the beach
and cross the road.

At the end of our drive
the neighbor's black cat meows
and sprawls for a scratch—
a sign of forgiveness,
perhaps even luck,

no junk in our mailbox to prove it,
pinetops giving sound to the wind,
the cat now rubbing my legs.
That sharp black tooth—
nothing I ever expected.

Window Washing

All activities have their shadow sides.
—Janwillem van de Wetering

I spray and wipe, standing back to spot
        those spots my father called *holidays*—
nothing festive or surprising to note,
        just a lapse that catches unawares,

a face on the shadowy glass, sullen
        for maybe a week, coming into focus.
Drag the blade, rub the image away,
        let that pine bough renumber its needles.

The pane squeaks. Birds have silenced themselves—
        a quiet so deep I can hear the fridge
click on downstairs, an urgent whisper
        from Phyllis calling me to the kitchen.

At the top of a dead pine, forty feet off,
        is a Cooper's hawk, not yet identified,
not until we take turns with the field guide
        and binoculars and read to each other

about the female's breast being white
        streaked with brown, just as this one is,
and how songbirds are high on her menu.
        Minutes stretch on without sound.

In the lenses it seems I could touch her
        where she sits for maybe ten minutes, letting
us look at the hooked beak and locked talons
        that hold me fast where I am—kitchen and

wife, everything gone. I am outside
        looking in at the man wearing glasses,

behind glass, making circles with a white rag,
        trying to rub anger away. I blink

and the branch is suddenly bare.
        Safely into other chores, I keep thinking
about chickadees, how fast, how they dart
        and swerve, how the book must be wrong.

Before dinner, the hawk reappears on our fence.
        I grab for the glasses. At first it seems
she's cleaning her feet, or ripping petals
        from a rose until the focus comes clear—

a black-capped head hanging down, and the Cooper's
        dark-pointed eyes making it hard to say
for a moment where I stand, hard to know
        whether I'm the seer or the one seen.

Witness

after a photo in The Best of LIFE

Faces that encircle
the boy and the fox
encircled a small woods

and moved the game
to this field of snow
cropped and tense,

black and white,
shaped by an idea
of time and space—

Holmes County, Ohio,
where a fox is cornered,
panting on black legs.

The tongue dangles
like a rag. Back legs
buckle; it squats

and squirts the snow
with terrified piss.
It does not see

the club, the boy
hatted like a batter
with a Little League grin.

His last two swings
have made two foxes
stiffen on the ground

like exclamation points ·
at his feet. No shadows.
The sun is elsewhere.

Family faces, expectant.
Smiles, mute cheers—
all behind him.

It is time; he steps
cautiously forward
like the crowd's one wish

cocking his long stick
in this paper place
of primal black

and white
where we must gather again
and again.

New Land

I'm still partly in Paris, stumbling
jet-lagged around this kitchen at dawn,
the shrill of Carolina cicadas
rising like that whistle of steam
from a kettle on the stove.

But when the house settles back
into silence, something is missing.
Minutes pass, and I know what it is—
that muffled *ponk   ponk   ponk*
heard most mornings before the air
is too hot to breathe.

Coffee in hand, I climb
to an upstairs window for this view
of three courts across the street,
and two men taking down nets,
rolling then stacking them up
by the white gazebo,

one old, one young,
now bending over long-handled scrapers,
working loose paint
from faint white perimeters,
the green surface faded and fissured.

A book I bought at Musée d'Orsay
shows Caillebotte's refinishers
on hands and knees,
bare to the waist, in a hot empty room,
like penitents sentenced to planes
that produce blond curls
from the long lacquered planks.

By midmorning an impression
of Chinese characters appears
in red on the green courts
by the younger man on hands and knees.
Bare to the waist, sweaty and bronzed,
he is cementing cracks with a red spackle.

Clouds with dark bellies swag
low over Bogue Sound,
close distance and flicker—brief silver
wires, sizzle and boom. But the men
spread green with a squeegee
and ease toward the gate where,
soaked, they retreat at last to their truck.

Later, I watch the young man
mix the acrylic with buckets of sand,
a thick pea soup that's sluiced
from a hundred-gallon barrel on wheels,
steered by the other
who waits in oak shade,
mopping his face with a red bandana
and watching the boy
bend a shirtless back to the sun.

At night, my windows glow
and pull me from desk and book
to see a dome of hazy brilliance
above the lit courts, almost finished,
quietly filling with emptiness
behind the wire diamonds of the fence.
Moths flicker in the lights, white
like the lines still missing,
or the naked woman
poised before notes on a silver stand,
violin to chin, ready to play.

Another Art

The art of horseshit isn't hard to master.
People crave some color along the way.
Besides, how could it lead to a disaster?

Start small. Tell her your love will last forever.
At first it's not an easy thing to say
But horseshit's not really hard to master.

Soon, though, you should take the whole thing further.
How once you dined with Cher and Doris Day.
Amazing. See? This leads to no disaster.

Then tell about the time that as a golfer
You hustled Lee Trevino, made him pay.
The art of horseshit isn't hard to master.

That scar? From Nam, when hunkered as a sniper,
You caught a bullet for a friend one day,
But, hey, you're still alive—no great disaster.

Until before a judge and talking faster,
Now sworn to tell the truth, you're forced to say
The art of horseshit isn't hard to master,
Though it leads to (I lied!) complete disaster.

Truant

When the weather is right,
on the long drive to work, country roads all the way,
I stop at a bridge

on the Neuse River
and walk the span to loosen my legs and check
the riverscape changing.

Five minutes might pass
before a car does. Last week, an old farmer idled by
on a green John Deere.

His passing opened a huge quiet.
High water chuckled against wooden piers.
Mayflies glittered in the sun.

And the watertop was a black trance
until a light blue kayak floated into view below me—
a kid with a blaze of blond hair.

He leaned back, paddle
across gunnels, blades flashing, his face to the sky,
an appraiser on duty.

With me it was a lake,
an Old Town canoe. I'd lie in the bottom, inspect the clouds
for shape, color, and size—my first job

to let the wind move me
toward some surprise, naming as I went: boot, nose, horsetail—
"Hey, are you okay?"

It was a county sheriff,
in a maroon cruiser, a white Stetson shading his face.
Did he think I was about to jump?

"You ain't got any ideas, right?"
I smiled and shook my head. *No ideas but in things,*
my smart-ass twin almost said.

But whatever ideas I had
had dissolved into a picture of that boy in the kayak
drifting with clouds.

"I was just looking," I said,
"Just looking," and stepped from the rail
toward one more hour at the wheel.

Spring on the Missouri

after Thomas Hart Benton

More trouble from the sky: a forked tongue
of lightning.
And the river out of its bed and rising,
backs of father and son bent
to loading the wagon for higher ground,
woodstove and mattress.

This has happened before: distant
thunder, then wind gusts, a whistle
growing shrill in shingles and cracks,
the creak of wood, then
a pattering like a plague of starlings
on the roof that drums and rumbles
day after day.

Fields lake up and seedlings go under.
Ma and Pa take turns sleeping
and keeping an eye
on the neighbor's white house growing
small in a glassy depth of field
as if floating away on the swift stream
not yet ready to crest.

Father and son must now be as fast,
folding a mattress into the yellowish wagon,
white wheels sunk in the rivering mud,
brown and white mules with ears straight up
as the lightning forks down
from one half of a soot-black sky,

the other half nearly sunny.
But the men are too busy to note
the tawny light,

or the robin's-egg blue
over the downriver sky, the unfair beauty
or the irony
of a simple white pitcher fallen in the mud
that one of the girls will jump
from the fleeing wagon to fetch.

Months from now,
always full of cold sweet water
from their well,
the pitcher will glow in the shack's half-light,
the same pitcher that will quench their thirst
on those long hot nights of the harvest.

Correspondence

"Congratulations on your book," she writes,
"but your excuses were always good stories."

And years from here,
you see a Lover's Lane by the railroad tracks,
or a teenage spot in the cemetery at Cedar Grove,
that world of upright stones, bare plunging
branches in gusty winds under a bad moon rising.

In high school you quit the marching band,
hocked your horn for a shotgun.
Saturday mornings ringnecks clattered up
into an air blue as denims.

Where you live now
football is played under lights
and above those distant trees, a cold brilliance.
Up the neighborhood street, starred with a lamp or two,
comes a boy in a white uniform
topped by a black-plumed shako.
He smiles and waves his trumpet,
grows small and disappears in a tunnel of dark,
moving to melodies,
buried phrases that need to be found.

Now you can see both ends of the street.

"P.S.," she writes, "Remember that Elvis tune,
beer in the bone orchard,
messing around,
shooting rats at the dump that night?"

Blue Water Report
to a Landlocked Friend

Holy Saturday. Our first trip out
to the Gulf Stream in this new season, 50 miles out
of our element—something that used to scare me,
a speck, under an immense inspecting sky
and all that moody water just waiting
for something to go wrong. But letting go
of land gets easier year after year.

We left in the dark,
my nephew on the bow with a spotlight
and hand signals to keep me from running aground
before we cleared the bar for deep water.
Damp cold until the sun climbed over the rim
and heated the cabin.

Nothing changes out of sight of land, you once said,
but the way clouds get brushed against blue
over the warm water of the Stream, those tints,
billows, tucks, and the definition that fades
the closer you come—a good argument
for never arriving.

But that would cancel the paintings
alive on the flanks of yellowfin, dorado, and wahoo—
especially dorado
with an iridescent dorsal,
blue dots, red and gold squiggles
that put me always in mind of Picasso or Gris,
and the way they glow like neon coming up to the transom.

Okay, here come the numbers.
The Stream was 80°
and the sonar read constant fish at 300 feet.

We boated five yellowfin in three hours, 50 pounds each.
On a double hookup, I took a rod
and the fight felt like pumping iron for half an hour
so I let the kid muscle in the rest.
From noon on there was nothing
until late afternoon, just before the run back in,
when a wahoo nailed our shotgun witch
and skied twice before he spit out the hook.

He was bigger than the yellowfin by far.
The kid's face collapsed.
But he already had five big ones in the fishbox,
and made me laugh by saying, "No sense being greedy."
True. Besides, we were only a few hours
from the chardonnay
and mesquite smoke of yum-yum city.

You're right, though, about trout,
excitement and relative size, that old joke
about equipment. Hell, Phyllis would agree—
her favorite sport is fishing up the spots and pins
we use to livebait for kings and cobia.
And catching two at a time
on 5-pound test *is* a thrill. Ask any kid
on the pier.

Remember when you first realized
there was no future in growing up?
Well, your kind of flycasting's beyond me now.
As a teenager, I took brookies,
but I've never learned the fine art of flies
and that's really the kind of fishing
that puts you in Walton's paradise
or takes away—
as the nuns used to say—
the temporal punishment due to sin,
that is, if you've abused your equipment
and end up in purgatorial flames.

Talk about letting go—on the way in,
running before a storm, I gave my nephew
the helm and the course heading and told him to wake me
when Lookout Light stood on the starboard,
which he did. When I came up from the cuddy,
the west was like a Turner
with that old wooden shrimper we saw stranded
on the shoals last fall
It's already been pounded to pieces. Only
a part of the wheelhouse sticks above white water
in the surf zone. Man, it doesn't take long. Hey,
keep your gear well oiled and ready to go.

PART II

At Encinitas

In a gallery on the beach
I'm stopped
by a steel sculpture—
a man harnessed

to a cart that an ox
might pull, the bulk
of it, heavy wheels
and wide steel rims,

the man leaning
as if into a hill,
legs and shoulders
muscled from years

without release,
the neck corded thick,
and the head—
faceless. Then

harness straps,
traces, high sideboards,
and inside: a huge face,
a meticulous mask,

bloated and vain,
lashed like a felon
to the bottom
of the cart.

Monkey Mind

The ocean's a wide plane of gleam and glint.
Sandpipers edge the surf, stab and dash,
     bring back that high school summer,
     under the raft with Rose Anne, touching—
Begin again.

The water's clear as air, green as Chinese tea.
The wind picks up.
Sand grains needle the skin.
     Mountains worn down, years in the billions—
Begin again.

A catsail tilts offshore.
Pelicans slide overhead—eight, nine, ten.
A ghost crab zips down its hole.
All legs, a girl stumbles from the surf, gleaming

     like Rose Anne, changing from her suit
     in the car's back seat, her—
Begin again.

A flight of sandpipers settles.
     Not a thought of Patagonia yet in their heads.
     Not a thought . . .

Cove Point

I nearly missed two grackles
touching off dazzle in a street puddle.
His face was getting in the way.

Earlier, I'd wanted the sweet sight
of a black eye, a few missing teeth,
his nose leaking blood

when through the window
a smooth sea had as much as said,
Hey, take a hike out to Cove Point.

I looked at the puddle again,
empty yet filled with his face,
my colleagues nodding yes

to his lopsided mouth. I was stuck
with that lying mug until tidal flats
appeared between live oaks,

then the Point, and a wide view.
On a bench in the onshore breeze,
I squinted at the sunpath,

sparkles strewn on the water
as if that grackle had been a preview
of brilliant distance,

vast stores of unused quiet.
I sat there,
filling with the sun-fired bay,

listening to the music of water,
the air cool on my skin.
A kingfisher hovered, then dove.

A bright snowy egret stilted
in slow motion
through the jade shallows.

Then someone shouted.
A yacht in the channel nearly collided
with an inbound skiff

hogging the narrows. The skipper
raised a fist he wouldn't have,
if the skiff had been empty and adrift.

On the cove's far side, guffaws
in the long shadows—some Chinese sage
laughing an eon away.

First Sight

His blond hair burning with sun,
I walk the empty beach with my neighbor's six-year-old.
The winter light is hard, our shadows sharp, black as tar.

Laughing gulls laugh
and wheel away before our feet sinking in sand
when we think we've heard
                              something
beyond the bar where mergansers dive,
something like rushing air that leads us farther east.

                  We hear it again
and when our eyes track and focus, it becomes a dolphin,
we think, before size revises upward to
                              a whale,
a pilot whale twenty feet long,
its black back glistening,
then down
with a great clap of its flukes.

We stop.
Winds are calm, no surf. We listen and look,
our lungs taken away
by the long loud bellows of his
and the sunstruck plume of mist standing for a moment
at his blowhole before he sinks out of sight,
and leaves us ankle-deep
in freezing tide, Benny now yelping
and splashing and ready
to follow the whole length of the island
until I call him back,
sense barely prevailing
in a riot of gulls laughing and diving
                              and wheeling in a purity
of blue and white overhead.

Plainsong Leavings

They had me waking
gladly for a change,
this family of wrens,
taking my first coffee
to the carport

for a peek inside
the watering can
shelved on its side,
four yellow beaks
opening and closing

then the black shine
of a mama's eye
in that mindful dark.
Fingers to lips,
smiling at each other,

my wife and I,
bowing like monks,
retreated inside
to a magnified quiet,
each house noise a song.

Too soon the nest
was a black hole, silence
replacing the three-note
shrill of mom and pop
on feeding runs.

Here one evening
the next morning gone.
We looked at each other,
then about the house,
shrubs, and trees—gone.

I lifted the can
and peered inside
at a snug cave crafted
of grass, reeds, leaves,
pine straw, string,

a strip of cellophane
and a clump of fur
from Blackie,
the cat next door.
I wondered:

How long did it take?
There's even a lip
to keep the littles
from falling out
but not from flying away.

Spiritsails

They are out there again,
kids from the church camp,
beyond the jetty, their sails

old-fashioned white,
a small fleet of spooks
learning how to tack, luff

and find the wind
when none seems there.
Spiritsail,

just yesterday I learned,
was the kind with a spar
that tips ahead of the mast

on old coastal schooners,
and it comes back now
through these white sails

that turn black
when backlit
on this blinding plain.

Way off to the right,
all by itself, one boat stalls,
then starts back,

you talking about an aunt
who passed over, a cousin as well.
I fill in the blanks

with faces of my own,
that one sail rejoining the rest.
Faint cries and shouts,

a melody of laughter borne
by an onshore breeze.
They merge and eclipse,

part on opposite headings
before they tack and jib
as if in a dance

beyond the black jagged rocks
of the jetty.

Oceania Fishing Pier

We're jigging for blues,
sunset doing its fiery fade, showy
as the tourist couple that ambles out,
all spiffed in summer whites,
glasses of zinfandel, hot for something to see.

And as if to please,
a guy gets a screamer strike on a live bait rig.
Now a twenty-pound cobia slaps the planks,
and the woman in white wrinkles her nose
with a line you might have predicted:

"He's not going to keep that poor thing, is he?"

Then it gets worse.
There's a trawler two hundred yards off the beach,
pulling nets through what's left of the sunpath,
a blizzard of gulls at the stern.

"So pretty," she says at my shoulder, "isn't it?"

No, it's *not* pretty, I want to say.
When you see a squall of gulls
behind a trawler on a sunset sea,
don't think beauty,
think bycatch: small blues and menhaden,
spots and croaker, unsellable mullet
littering the surface for acres,
feeding the gulls.
Think trawl doors that plow the bottom,
kill coral, fill the crannies
and hiding holes for next year's fry.
Think analogy:
harvesting corn with a bulldozer.

Pretty still echoes in the air,
and she *is* too.
Lips glistening with wine, she asks
if all this ain't as pretty as a postcard?

Looking down at the cobia opening
and closing its mouth, dying, slowly
dying, I tell her it is.

Wrasse

The ocean has a perfect memory
of who you are,
salt calling to salt, water to water,
and strips you
of family, job, and address
as quickly as you click the dive watch,
check the p.s.i., dump air
and ease down the anchor rope,
equalizing into the deep
blue world of waver and drift.

Three years and six stories down,
the *Indra* has started to ripen,
her steel gone orange with rust,
a long slow waving of kelp,
railings fuzzy but sharp
with urchins and barnacle rosettes,
quills that could inflate a finger
to twice its size.
Below decks, prison-striped spadefish
have made the passageway theirs,
the shower stalls too where hex
tile glows in your dive light.

A four-foot barracuda by the bridge
circles more tightly
with that overbite smile,
darts and veers from your mask
at the last moment
to remind you how dreams need
to flex and test,
how angels   butterflies,
   blue hamlets   and tangs
need crevice and crack,
how open water would turn them to snacks,

but not this wrasse,
yellow and no larger than a long finger.

A great grouper, amberjack, and sea bass
all wait in a loose congregation,
for his favors on the top deck
where clutches of tube worms
sway in the underwater wind,
opening and closing.

The way he bumps and frisks over each body
you'd think he was a narc.
The grouper keeps open its cave
of a mouth and he swims right in.
An impatient jack,
pectorals aflicker, holds
for its turn by a bulkhead.
Under a frail peace, this yellow beauty
holds them apart and keeps them waiting
as he gets at tiny crustaceans,
lice, worms, and bits of dead skin,
slides into their gills
and into the face of every last one,
no matter how large or toothy.

You release the air in your vest,
settle on the deck like a Buddha,
practice your breathing,
and watch the wrasse do its work,
each breath brightening colors
that could flower at the top
of this chain of bubbles rising.

Line Squall

I had forgotten it again,
the *it* that is always,
Gensha says,
to be used
and slides like invisible thread
through the slightest moments
until the picture
window put me in mind:

a wedge of weather
in fast advance,
clouds on the boil,
the sunny ocean
going green, indigo,
and black again

with a staggered line
of white ibis
languidly rowing
right to left,
their long necks
arrowed away
and unaware
of invisible thread
or the air
flickering like welding
in high school shop,
something on the build
and emerging
with sandspit islands exposed
one after another
by the outgoing tide
and a smoke-blue heron,

tall spirit
of the shallows,
always alert.

Hurricane Warning: Surfers

Around the bend slides an ocean eerie with storm light
and them at serious play: red and yellow wet suits, blue

and lime, their unconcern a reminder of something
long forgotten but now too strong to let go. Wind tugs

our pants and sleeves and has our hair fly back like spume
from the crests of fifteen footers rolling in. We lean

against the wind and hear the fringe of pampas grass
threshing above the beach where these boys worry

not a jot for tomorrow and make light of leaden swells—
a dream of Waimea Bay and the ache of endless summer

come at last to the Carolinas. Oblivious of snapping red flags,
riptides and undertows, they wait and wait for one moment

to lift them, a force evolving shape within us, making us
wait too, smile when the curl flexes and tilts them ahead

toward a lethal bottom of sand. How they tame the edge,
gravity giving way to a grace of their own making!

Some miss the moment and wait still, and when we leave
the island, exiled inland, I'm not even thinking of our house

turned to matchwood. Days later, through sweaty hours
of shingle and tack, chainsaw and tree limb, I still see

that boy farthest out, the one waiting past friends, now up
in one motion, his wetsuit blazing orange, ready to defy all ruin.

Pennywort, After the Storm

Coming back along the boardwalk,
buckled in places,
over dunes,
over those discs struck silver by the sun,
even before we hit the parking lot
and you brightened like a kid at the two
new pennies nobody wanted
to stoop for,
I was still thinking
about the newly minted scatter—
how stubbornly they thrive in white sand,
a whole trove of green
coins spilling down the side of the dune.

Today's Weather Is Brought to You by . . .

Before that hot wind all the way from the African coast
churned into a house-flattening force
leaving the island a look worse than winter,
more shingles on roads than roofs,
a friend came back from a walk oblivious,
bite welts blooming on her arms and neck,
her eyes lit: "You're lucky,"
she said, "You've got painted buntings by the marsh."

And out came the field guide:
metallic blue head, scarlet breast, patches of yellow
and green—truly a work of paint
at one remove, a feathered beauty
most birders would brave more than bites
to list. But that vivid color
and natural history came right into the comfort
of our cool front room.
No sticky heat, no low-tide stink, bites, or sound. Nothing

like the morning
police made us leave
with the boom of ten-foot combers in our ears,
flying foam, our faces wet, salt on the tongue
and what we felt—
nothing as safe or small
as what we saw on Channel 12 that night
in a school gym far from home.

Once back on the island, we saw
wind had ripped the curtain of leaves to something
like a shrimper's net, holes letting in
the sea's blue distance, coloring what was close
an unfamiliar hue. After cleanup one day,
over by the swamp,

oak and pine flattened to a black profile,
we saw for an instant
a cutout bunting that, colorless,
didn't quite count. But mornings now
when the wind is right and brings us a faint song,
we head for the marsh hoping to see
those vivid colors
for ourselves.

Fog Lifter

Mornings I walk myself awake,
usually after the boats start up
and work their way to sea.

Bogue Sound, by the time I stumble
across the island's one road,
busy with cars, and come to it

over the boardwalk that jogs
across the salt marsh to a view,
is still again, so calm and polished

that the snarl of an outboard or slap
of a wave would seem a violence.
But there is none, not now.

Instead there are flute notes filling
the salt air with no one in sight.
It has to be a dream prop, I guess,

this music stand by itself
at the end of the pier, a page
of notes with Mozart's name,

as if the player were invisible.
But she's sitting on the lowest stair,
just above the water,

a girl with blond hair charming
the scene to a graceful trance
while her family sleeps in a rental

by the roar of surf on the beach.
Her back to me, she plays on
and on, her body swaying

as I watch the sun climb higher,
fog lifting from trees and houses
on the far side at Spooner's Creek.

For the Woman at the Dock Who Asked What It Was Like Down There

Like easing out of the body
into sleep or love, no need for words
to rise toward the quicksilver surface,
rising on a waver of light from the *Atlas*, a tanker
eighty feet down

Like the difference between light
and the weight you feel
when you first hit the deck shedding water,
mask, fins, belt, and tank,
almost light again

Like drifting off, our moonlit wet suits
swimming in place on the cord between porch posts,
lighter still in the onshore breeze, drying,
becoming lighter,
loose-limbed and hovering
behind dunes swaying with sea oats. . . .

Then ghosting again
among queen angels and blue parrots
chromis and clouds of spot-tail pins gliding
by encrusted rails   horned cleats and sea doors
at ease among anemones
on the tanker wreck   this great garden of rust

PART III

Dusk Watch

in memoriam Bodo Nischan

We were sitting on the roof deck,
four friends with a bottle,
maybe six months after he died,

low sun melting on an emptiness
of ocean, waves almost quiet,
when into view floated a line

of brown pelicans,
hedge clippers with wings,
more than a dozen

in a slow-motion glide
along a curving sickle of sand
suddenly veering,

wings motionless, fixed,
as if we were in somebody's sights,
Gerda saying they were his favorites—

characters comic
and soulful at the same time. Then,
as if called, one bird

left the cortège and returned,
turned tightly over the roof
four or five times,

the last an eye-level pass
before he angled off
to follow that long dark line.

We looked at each other
and finally laughed, Gerda too,
her eyes wide and wet.

We felt the wind
pick up, saw waves whiten,
but until the water went black

and the bottle was empty
we went on talking, nobody
saying a word.

Winter

after Andrew Wyeth

It begins in a cold upper room
windowing the blank expanse of Kuerner's Hill,
his father not long in the ground, killed
by a train,
when this boy comes running,
a dark-brown apparition, one arm drifting free,
the other frozen, an erratic figure
pitched down the steep mound of earth.
No sky or clouds, no high colors.
Blue of pie berries as forgotten as summer.
Only thin sunlight to blacken the turf
with a long shadow
stuck like flames to his fleeing heels.

It will be winter now, always
a process of separating muted color
from the earthdark his father has become—
dun and ocher, gray and black;
whites as cold as snow.
No Frenchy greens or reds,
just murky firs, a dull brick farmhouse wall,
a blue barn door,
a geranium like an ember in the woodstove dark.
Even in the summer of *Christina's World*
it is winter, grasses of the long rise
parched and bleached, the woman sprawled
in a pink so faded it's nearly white, abandoned

like this boy—earflaps wild in the wind.
He is crossing
ghost tracks of a farm truck
that climb the hill past patches of snow,

fence posts, bare brush fringing the top
toward a deadly crossing hidden on the other side
where trains still wail without warning.

How to Deal with Early Dark

First consider your mood,
the direction memory is likely to move.
This is preparation for nothing but itself.
Consider color and tempo, how you want to process
a silence that darkens and builds.
Mozart or Mingus?

Take your time at the window
with the last orange light on the black bones of trees.
This will help you decide.
Let there be enough volume to reach the kitchen
and the Maker's Mark, 80 proof—
less potent but better for its first lively sting.

Uncap, and breathe in the blue bass chords
that blossom in the low light.
Take the one glass saved from your parents' crystal,
allow them entrance
along with other lost faces from the past.

Pour two ounces, clunk in some cubes
and a splash of Poland Spring.
Savor the smoky bite of that first baritone ride.
Now lean back in your best chair
and listen, just listen.

Eventide

When you round Cove Point, the sun,
like a low red host, has migrated
west of the church steeple

over an anchorage of sloops and ketches
into what will soon be night
past the carcass

of a skiff almost hidden in the weeds.
You set down your bucket,
remove your sandals

and wade in with your net, just like the boy
last fall. He was happy
to show you

how to untangle the skirt, hold hemmed weights,
one between the front teeth, others
in your right hand.

Then you try to toss it into a full circle bloom
and discover that casting
a wide net isn't easy.

Hauling now, you feel a resistance, something
as needed as the ceremonial white scatter
of ibis farther out.

Menhaden and mullet wrinkle the surface
but shrimp stay hidden until a full net
gently thumps on retrieve.

Bead eyes, see-through bodies,
five black dots, four on the tail blades,
one for a heart.

Church bells ring against the rapt quiet.
Extra ecclesiam nulla salus sounds
from the past,

but the west is a great panel of stained glass
in this huge cathedral of air.

Fox

Home from work, you slip off shoes and sink into the sofa
        with office news I try to hear, but can't
wait to tell about the fox that came right up to our door.

Bear, fox, bobcat, that swamp owl out back hooting
        hi-lo's at twilight—you've heard
these variations so many times you begin to laugh,

which is good, because I'm always half-swacked on animals,
        this morning half-asleep when something
made me look outside as he emerged from mist by the shed.

On black forelegs, he moved ahead, slowly, toward another
        fox in the glass door where I crouched, as still
as I could. What brought him so close? I remembered mice

tracks in snow, and trails under the house where I've crawled
        to run speaker wire between rooms. Now just
feet away, I must have come into focus, blinked, or moved.

He stopped and stood, not quite still, but not frozen either.
        Wise narrow-eyed face, black nose twitching.
His thin red flanks inflated with each breath of my own,

eyes peering into our den, maybe at mine. In that long look
        I felt an exchange. When I was a boy,
the bounty was five bucks. Poor country kids, we all did it.

Breathless, I tried to lengthen the moment before it faltered
        and he was gone like smoke into smoke,
that moment giving shape to the day, and you arriving,

of course, igniting this need to tell about something hunted
        past words, those images we saw in France

where small human hunters once through pipes blew pigment
onto cave walls and shaped the creatures that kept them alive.

Utah, Nine-Mile Canyon

It's a petroglyph not easy to find, pecked out
of redrock near a riverbed strewn with boulders,

hidden in an overhang you could hike past
if you weren't looking for this hunter panel

you heard about from a friend
who sketched a map and promised a place

to take you back to beginnings. And there it was,
still is, lower in the alcove than imagined,

lighting the gallery of your mind against twilight,
snow coming down, fire dying, brandy gone.

From simple lines: fabulous hunters, shaman
at the side, bows drawn and arrows nocked.

They are inching toward elk. On the right, creeping
closer is the man in a big-horn headdress,

closer to the promise that merges seer with seen,
hunter and hunted, ten centuries gone tonight.

Prey

Coming from the pool
where I've just done laps, letting water bring me back,
I'm already elsewhere, thinking
about Tennyson and my two o'clock class
when a squirrel appears
ten feet from the concrete walk, by an oak.

Then a loud ruffle at my shoulder,
like an umbrella unfurled, before a flash glide
makes the red-tail seem to emerge from *me*

and nail the squirrel with a clatter of wings—
a long scream that strips varnish from my heart
before the sound goes limp.

She presides with mantling wings
over the last twitches of gray as I
edge closer to her golden eye.
She hackles her head feathers, tightens her talons,

holds me prey to what I see, watches me
as she lifts off, rowing hard for height, the squirrel
drooped in her clutch.

Now skimming a lake
of cartops in the south lot, making for the break
between Wendy's and Kinko's, she swerves up

sharply to land on the roofpeak of a frat house
over on Tenth.

Some noise from the world snaps me back.
I look about, but nobody has stopped
to look at me or where she stood by the tree,

only ten feet away. Slowly released,
I move ahead with the passing student crowd,
holding fast to what I have seen.

Wild

We're walking into blue light,
a moon lifting from Bogue Sound,
in no hurry toward the docks,
closer to the shouting
of a couple

on the far side of the cove,
him always hurting
her goddamn feelings.
For years. Then a loud slap
from the back screen door.

When hand over hand
I hoist the trap,
they scuttle, climb and cling
to the black wire diamonds,
upside down, undersides white,

the spine and V-bones
of the rock bass bait they have laid bare
and white as sand.
One by one, when I shake the trap,
these blue claws thump

into the plastic bucket
where they scrabble, click, and lock claws.
We stand on the dock
and breathe the thick wild air,
sharp as the doubles of stars

we stand among
wavering on the surface
of what we can barely fathom.

Last Call

William Matthews (1941–1997)

He answered the phone uncertainly,
long distance dark between us,

and the sound of caught breath,
wheezing, then a drawn-out silence.

I asked if anything was wrong.
He coughed and said he'd been alone

in his apartment all day, watching
the snow fly, listening to jazz,

feeling something slowly grow inside.
"Your phone call did it," he said.

"When I opened my mouth just now,
a huge hawk moth fluttered out."

I knew better than to ask further.
I see it still beating at the overhead light.

Needs

My mother could only sigh
at his need for gags—
the flyaway dollar, the dribble glass,
fake turds on the carpet.
And I was my father's son, she said.
Ever since high school
I've enjoyed tapping the wrong shoulder
so the person turns
to empty space
or the face of some stranger.
I play it now on my son.

On his last visit
my father came alone for the first time.
I waited in the arrivals lounge
and scanned a parade of faces,
each one not his,
sure something dire
had happened in Newark.
Then someone taps my shoulder,
but no one's there
before I face him
in fake glasses, rubber nose, and wig.
I sighed—it's true—my mother's role
now mine.

My father gone,
I feel that tap again today,
alone at the mall,
and turn to the huge empty air
slowly filled
with a white wall, blank as paper,
then a ghost
hidden in the laugh-wrinkled
face of my son.

Tight

Two of our table chairs
wobble when sat on,
she says,
or haven't I noticed
those wooden groans?
I turn them upside down
and see the years,
how they've loosened
high backs from seats
and mitered braces,
screws with no bite
in widened holes.
I'm looking at separation,
thinking
about thicker screws,
about switching to inch,
maybe inch and a half,
when my father
and his trick appear
out of a dark nowhere:
toothpicks or
a matchstick
depending on the size
of the hole
that seems to grow larger
the closer I look,
an everyday small black hole.
I go with a matchstick,
slide it in,
then the screw,
then turn to happy resistance,
the squeak of dry wood
the tighter I turn,
the black crack closing

to a mahogany seam
and we're tight again.
I wink at Phyllis, laugh,
and tap my Polack temple
just as my father did.

Lac d'Aiguebelette

With its fresh blood and pissed-on cobbles
Paris is finally far to the west,
nearly absolved, we think,
in these clear waters
that reprint clouds and peaks
with no bias.

La dent du chat overhead,
             jutting last tooth of the Jura,
the right place for a swim,
so we ease down the riprap, my son and I,
remove our shorts, and tumble in,
trying to forget that Parisian street,
a man in a burnoose
lying in a lake of blood
off *La rue du chat qui pêche.*

Fish and sin—words
that sound about the same in French,
but make no connection.
Cats that fish, men that sin.
Sometimes the story can never be known.
Why bother to fish?

This mountain water is first
like a blade going in, a numbness,
then a slowing of breath.
We float on our backs,
that cold sharp tooth gleaming above us.

Into the Frame

You hike through a tunnel of live oak,
cool shade and wren song,

then climb the stairs that top out
on a high dune strewn with pennywort.

The sudden ocean and opening sky
make everything dizzy and unreal.

Like brightness after matinees
and those long treks home with friends.

But stop. Let this place erase everything
but itself, water a turquoise radiance,

sand a whiteness that stuns.
Just watch the young flood rushing

over ribs and welts, carving
new channels, mocking the known.

In the distance a red-and-yellow sail,
black patches on the water from clouds.

At your feet, a peach-colored canopy,
a man in a low chair lost in a book

and teens on a blanket lost in each other.
A father and son playing catch.

Middle distance, behind the bar, a boy
with blond hair and blue pail follows

a surge channel, an oxbow bending,
down the beach and out to open water.

He seems to be playing a secret game,
whispering, conjuring flow in the channel.

It's all like a painting, space between figures,
sun making sharp shadows, dramatic

clouds on the move, when into the picture,
in clear water, near the boy,

a dark mass like a shadow with silver glints,
an inky form that billows and compresses

but holds a shape—a school of finger mullet
trying to fool a longer lean shadow

that darts and swerves like the peregrine
you saw once stoop into a flock of starlings.

The boy sees it too, drops his blue pail,
and turns to call. Nobody is looking but you,

a hidden god who sees no need to intrude—
the fish a toothless cobia, not a shark,

now stuck in the oxbow unable to turn
at the low end, but the boy stoops,

as you want him to, and scoots it
over the shelf, then stands to watch

it clear and disappear
into deeper water with a lash of its tail.

No one, for once, shouted *Shark!*
Now the boy turns with what he has seen

to the father and brother playing catch,
the man in tent shade lost in his book.

The scene becomes a painting again.
Go ahead. Step into the frame,

descend one step at a time
to all that white sand, jade and windy light,

the boy still in you, latent but not lost,
running to tell you his tale.

Roofers

Across the street, houses
are still black shapes, the ocean
turning amber in between,

then orange after coffee
and toast, red with the mayhem
of headlines that stop

at a first beating of hammers.
Three of them move around the roof,
around a Gatorade keg,

toting rolls of tar paper,
bent sideways with buckets of sealer.
A kid with long blond hair

shovels the shingles
that flap from the edge of the roof.
I bring him close with binoculars,

watch them rag the small guy—
Shorty from years ago,
whose answer was to grab his crotch.

Talk is the same—cars, women,
and getting high (an eye
out for the foreman's blue pickup),

the paycheck pool, a hot tip
on the fifth race at Lincoln—
the weekend just hours away.

The blond kid climbs to the peak.
He pulls off his shirt,
and hunkers down to a smoke.

A shrimper pulling nets
in a storm of gulls
keeps appearing between houses.

This room disappears.
Clouds drift seaward. Hands still black
from the tar kettle, no ambition,

I watch what comes into view,
always eager for the small good thing
that happens next.

Acknowledgments

Grateful acknowledgment is made to editors of the following publications in which some of these poems or earlier versions of them first appeared:

The American Scholar: "Needs",

Dos Passos Review: "How to Deal with Early Dark";

Garbanzo.com: "Another Art";

The Hampden-Sydney Poetry Review: "Departures";

The Hudson Review: "Dusk Watch," "Eventide," "Into the Frame," "Line Squall," "Off-Season," "Oceania Fishing Pier," "Tight";

The Louisville Review: "Monkey Mind";

NEO: "Cove Point," "Plainsong Leavings," "Promised Land," "Wild," "Window Washing";

The News & Observer: "Spiritsails";

North American Review: "Truant";

Orion: "Last Call," "Today's Weather Report Is Brought to You by . . .";

Poet & Critic: "Correspondence";

Poet Lore: "Roofers";

Poetry: "Hurricane Warning," "Pennywort: After the Storm," "Spring on the Missouri";

Prairie Schooner: "Fox";

Rattle: "For the Woman at the Dock Who Asked What It Was Like Down There";

The Sewanee Review: "Dominion," "Empty Air," "First Sight," "New Land," "Portside Marina";

Southern Poetry Review: "At Encinitas," "Blue Water Report to a Land-locked Friend," "Lac d'Aiguebelette";

The Southern Review: "Fog Lifter," "Wrasse."

"Prey" originally appeared in *Urban Nature: Poems About Wild Life in the City,* edited by Laure-Anne Bosselaar, Milkweed Editions, 2000.

"Winter" originally appeared in *The Store of Joys: Writers Celebrate North Carolina Museum of Art's Fiftieth Anniversary,* edited by Huston Paschal, John F. Blair, Publisher, 1997.

"Last Call" appeared in *Blues for Bill: A Tribute to William Matthews,* edited by Kurt Brown, Meg Kearney, Donna Reis, and Estha Weiner (University of Akron Press, 2005).

"At Encinitas," "Into the Frame," "New Land," "Off-Season," "Spring on the Missouri," "Utah, Nine-Mile Canyon," and "Winter" were first collected and published with other poems as a chapbook entitled *Into the Frame* (Independent Press, 2004).

About the Author

Peter Makuck is Distinguished Professor of Arts and Sciences at East Carolina University where he has edited *Tar River Poetry* since 1978. He has published three collections of poetry including *Where We Live* (BOA Editions, 1982), *The Sunken Lightship* (BOA Editions, 1990), and *Against Distance* (BOA Editions, 1997), three poetry chapbooks, two collections of short stories, and co-edited a book of essays, *An Open World,* on the Welsh poet Leslie Norris. His most recent book of short stories, *Costly Habits* (University of Missouri Press, 2002), was nominated for a PEN/Faulkner Award. In 1988 he was the recipient of the Brockman Award, given annually for the best collection of poetry by a North Carolinian, and the Charity Randall Citation from the International Poetry Forum. His essays, reviews, stories, and poems have appeared in *The Hudson Review, The Sewanee Review, Poetry,* and *The Laurel Review.* With his wife Phyllis, he lives on Bogue Banks, one of North Carolina's barrier islands.

BOA EDITIONS, LTD., AMERICAN POETS CONTINUUM SERIES

Colophon

Off-Season in the Promised Land, poems by Peter Makuck,
was set in Garamond by Richard Foerster, York Beach, Maine.
The cover design is by Daphne Poulin-Stofer;
the cover photograph, by Justin Brett.
Manufacturing was by McNaughton & Gunn, Lithographers,
Saline, Michigan.

The publication of this book was made possible, in part,
by the special support of the following individuals:

Alan & Nancy Cameros
Gwen & Gary Conners
Burch & Louise Craig
Susan DeWitt Davie
Bradley P. & Debra Kang Dean
Leaf Drake
Suzanne & Peter Durant
Dr. Henry & Beverly French
Dane & Judy Gordon
Kip & Deb Hale
Tom & Peggy Hubbard
Peter & Robin Hursh
Robert & Willy Hursh
Archie & Pat Kutz
Rosemary & Lewis Lloyd
Barbara & John Lovenheim
Boo Poulin
Deborah Ronnen
Sue S. Stewart
Thomas R. Ward
Pat & Michael Wilder
Glenn & Helen William